Other Books by
RICHARD BRAUTIGAN

Richard Brautigan

Loading Mercury
with a Pitchfork

Simon and Schuster   New York

Published by Simon and Schuster
A Gulf+Western Company
Rockefeller Center, 630 Fifth Avenue
New York, New York 10020

Designed by Elizabeth Woll
Manufactured in the United States of America
1   2   3   4   5   6   7   8   9   10

Library of Congress Cataloging in Publication Data

Brautigan, Richard.
   Loading mercury with a pitchfork.

   I. Title.
PS3503.R2736L6   811'.5'4   76-2001
ISBN 0-671-22263-5
ISBN 0-671-22271-6 pbk.

Some of these poems first appeared in *Mademoiselle, Harper's Magazine, Blue Suede Shoes, The World, Mark in Time, California Living, Five Poems* (Serendipity Books), *Esquire, Clear Creek, City Lights Anthology,* and *The CoEvolution Quarterly*

For Jim Harrison and Guy de la Valdene
"Friendship"

CONTENTS

CROWS AND MERCURY

POSTCARD

I wonder if eighty-four-year-old Colonel Sanders
ever gets tired of travelling all around America
    talking about fried chicken.

LOADING MERCURY WITH A PITCHFORK

Loading mercury with a pitchfork
your truck is almost full. The neighbors
take a certain pride in you. They
    stand around watching.

IT'S TIME TO TRAIN YOURSELF

It's time to train yourself
to sleep alone again
and it's so fucking hard.

THE ACT OF:
DEATH-DEFYING AFFECTION

The act of: death-defying affection
insures the constancy of the stars
and their place at the beginning of
everything.

TWO GUYS GET OUT OF A CAR

Two guys get out of a car.
They stand beside it. They
don't know what else to do.

PUNITIVE GHOSTS LIKE STEAM-DRIVEN TENNIS COURTS

Punitive ghosts like steam-driven tennis courts
haunt the apples in my nonexistent orchard.
I remember when there were just worms out there
and they danced in moonlit cores on warm September
     nights.

CROW MAIDEN

Starring a beautiful young girl and twenty-three crows. She has blonde hair. The crows are intelligent. The director is obsessed with the budget (too low). The photographer has fallen in love with the girl. She can't stand him. The crows are patient. The director is a homosexual. The girl loves him. The photographer daydreams murder. "One hundred and seventy-five thousand. I was a fool!" the director says to himself. The girl has taken to crying a lot at night. The crows wait for their big scene.

And you will go where crows go
and you will know what crows know.

After you have learned all their secrets
and think the way they do and your love
caresses their feathers like the walls
of a midnight clock, they will fly away
and take you with them.

And you will go where crows go
and you will know what crows know.

INFORMATION

Any thought that I have right now
isn't worth a shit because I'm totally
fucked up.

ARE YOU THE LAMB OF
YOUR OWN FORGIVING?

I mean: Can you forgive yourself / all
   those crimes without victims?

AUTOBIOGRAPHY (POLISH IT
LIKE A PIECE OF SILVER

I am standing in the cemetery at Byrds, Texas.
What did Judy say? "God-forsaken is beautiful, too."
A very old man, who has cancer on his face and takes
care of the cemetery, is raking a grave in such a
manner as to almost (polish it like a piece of silver.
An old dog stands beside him. It's a hot day: 105.
What am I doing out here in west Texas, standing in
a cemetery? The old man wonders about that, too.
My presence has become a part of his raking. I know
that he is also polishing me.

AUTOBIOGRAPHY (WHEN THE MOON SHINES LIKE A DEAD GARAGE

When the moon shines like a dead garage
I travel with gasoline ghosts down all those haunted
miles of the past, twenty-seven Model A miles an hour
in 1939, going to where I have forgotten.

AUTOBIOGRAPHY (GOOD-BYE, ULTRA VIOLET

The telephone rings in San Francisco,
        "This is Ultra Violet."
I don't know her except that she
is a movie actress.
She wants to talk to me.
She has a nice voice.
We talk for a while.
Then she has to go someplace.
        "Good-bye."

JANUARY ⚡ 3

I've started off with a mistake
but I'll try to get better
and put the day in good order.

THEY ARE REALLY HAVING FUN

They are really having fun,
        drinking glasses of wine
and talking about things
        that they like.

WE MEET. WE TRY. NOTHING HAPPENS, BUT

We meet. We try. Nothing happens, but
afterwards we are always embarrassed
when we see each other. We look away.

HOME AGAIN HOME AGAIN
LIKE A TURTLE TO HIS BALCONY

Home again home again like a turtle to his balcony
and you know where that's at.

YOU WILL HAVE UNREAL
RECOLLECTIONS OF ME

(For Rilke)

You will have unreal recollections of me
like half-developed photographs
for all the days of your life, even though
you have never met me because I have dreamt
you. Soon it will be morning, the dream
over.

FINDING IS LOSING SOMETHING ELSE

Finding is losing something else.
I think about, perhaps even mourn,
    what I lost to find this.

IMPASSE

I talked a good hello
but she talked an even
     better good-bye.

HOMAGE TO CHARLES ATLAS

A daydream exercises your mind
for a moment or two like an invisible
muscle. Then it's gone, totally
    forgotten.

ON PURE SUDDEN DAYS LIKE INNOCENCE

On pure sudden days like innocence
we behold the saints and their priorities
   keypunched in the air.

CURIOUSLY YOUNG LIKE A FRESHLY-DUG GRAVE

Curiously young like a freshly-dug grave
the day parades in circles like a top
     with rain falling in its shadow.

RIGHT BESIDE THE MORNING COFFEE

If I write this down now, I
will have it in the morning.
The question is: Do I want
to start the day off with
        this?

MONTANA INVENTORY

At 85 miles an hour an insect splattered
like saffron on the windshield
and a white cloud in blue sky above the
    speed-curried bug

OAK

crows / the
crows / the
(the tree)

BEN

I telephone Oklahoma this evening. The telephone
rings eight or nine times but nobody's home. Ben's
not in his trailer parked in a field just outside
　　　of Oklahoma City.

THE NECESSITY OF APPEARING
IN YOUR OWN FACE

There are days when that is the last place
in the world where you want to be but you
have to be there, like a movie, because it
            features you.

FOR FEAR YOU WILL BE ALONE

For fear you will be alone
you do so many things
that aren't you at all.

WAR HORSE

He stands alone in a pasture
but nobody can see him.

He has been made invisible
by his own wounds.

I know how he feels.

ALBERT EINSTEIN (OR UPON
FIRST READING THAT LIGHT IS
PROJECTING ITSELF AT
372,000 MILES PER SECOND FROM
CRAB NEBULA 5,000 OLD-FASHIONED
LIGHT-YEARS AWAY

We all lose a few.

"GOOD WORK," HE SAID, AND

"Good work," he said, and
went out the door. What
work? We never saw him
before. There was no door.

LOVE

SEPTEMBER 3
(THE DR. WILLIAM CARLOS WILLIAMS MISTAKE

I had severe insomnia last night with
the past, the present and the future detailing
        themselves
like: Oh, the shit we run through our minds!
Then I remembered that it was Dr. William Carlos
Williams' birthday and that made me feel better
        until almost dawn.

        Note:

        *September 3 is not
        Dr. William Carlos Williams'
        birthday. It is the birthday
        of a girlfriend.
        Dr. William Carlos Williams
        was born on September 17, 1883.*

        Interesting mistake.

LIGHTHOUSE

Signalling, we touch,
lying beside each other
       like waves.
I roll over into her
and look down through
candlelight to say,
"Hey, I'm balling you."

EVERYTHING INCLUDES US

The thought of her hands
        touching his hair
makes me want to vomit.

WHAT HAPPENED?

You were the prettiest girl
in your high school graduating class
       in 1927.

Now you have short blue hair
and nobody loves you,
not even your own children.

They don't like to have you around
because you make them nervous.

I'LL AFFECT YOU SLOWLY

I'll affect you slowly
as if you were having
a picnic in a dream.
There will be no ants.
     It won't rain.

UMBRELLAING HERSELF LIKE A POORLY-DESIGNED ANGEL

Umbrellaing herself like a poorly-designed angel
she falls in love again: destined to a broken heart
which is the way it always is for her. I'm glad
she's not falling in love with me.

HERE IS SOMETHING BEAUTIFUL (ETC.

Here is something beautiful (etc.
I have so little left that you
        would want.
Its color begins in your hand.
Its shape is your touch.

AS MECHANICAL AS A FLIGHT OF STAIRS

As mechanical as a flight of stairs,
as solemn as a flight of stairs,
they have found each other after years
      of looking.

WE WERE THE ELEVEN O'CLOCK NEWS

We were the eleven o'clock news
because while the rest of the world
was going to hell we made love.

AT THE GUESS OF A SIMPLE HELLO

At the guess of a simple hello
    it can all begin
toward crying yourself to sleep,
wondering where the fuck
    she is.

SEXUAL ACCIDENT

The sexual accident
that turned out to be your wife,
the mother of your children
and the end of your life, is home
cooking dinner for all your friends.

BUSINESS

When he died he left his wife
three gas stations and a warehouse.
He left his mistress two supermarkets.

FUCK ME LIKE FRIED POTATOES

Fuck me like fried potatoes
on the most beautifully hungry
morning of my God-damn life.

FLOWERS FOR A CROW

You have your friends.
  I have mine.

SECTION 3

HAVE YOU EVER BEEN THERE?

I can tell by your eyes that I
have asked the wrong question.
They look troubled and away. We'll
        change the subject.

ATTILA AT THE GATES
OF THE TELEPHONE COMPANY

They said that
my telephone
would be fixed
     by 6.
They guaranteed
     it.

THE AMELIA EARHART PANCAKE

I have been unable to find a poem
for this title. I've spent years
looking for one and now I'm giving
        up.
                    November 3, 1970

I DON'T WANT TO KNOW ABOUT IT

I don't want to know about it.
Tell it to somebody else.
They'll understand and make you
     feel better.

MARCH 18, RESTING IN THE MAYTAG HOMAGE

Looking out a hotel window
it's snowing in New York with
great huge snowflakes like millions
of transparent washing machines swirling
through the dirty air of this city, washing
      it.

WE ARE IN A KITCHEN

We are in a kitchen
in Santa Fe, New Mexico.
Some bacon is frying.
It smells like a character
that you like in a good movie.
A beautiful girl is watching
        the bacon.

THE LAST SURPRISE

The last surprise is when you come
gradually to realize that nothing
        surprises you any more.

TOWARD THE PLEASURES OF
A RECONSTITUTED CROW

Toward the pleasures of a reconstituted crow
I collect darkness within myself like the shadow
    of a blind lighthouse.

A MOTH IN TUCSON, ARIZONA

A friend calls me on the telephone
from Tucson, Arizona. He's unhappy.
He wants to talk to somebody
          in San Francisco.
We talk for a while. He mentions
there's a moth in the room.
          "It's solemn," he says.

DEATH LIKE A NEEDLE

Death like a needle
made from a drunken clown's breath
sews the shadow of a [I can't make
the next two words out. I first
wrote this poem in longhand] to your
      shadow.

HEROINE OF THE TIME MACHINE

When she was fifteen if you'd told her
that when she was twenty she'd be going
to bed with bald-headed men and liking it,
she would have thought you very abstract.

IT TAKES A SECRET TO KNOW A "SECRET"

It takes a secret to know a "secret."
Then you have two secrets that know
        each other. Just
what you always wanted, they stand
there looking at each other with their
        pajamas on.

VOLUNTARY QUICKSAND

I read the *Chronicle* this morning
as if I were stepping into voluntary
        quicksand
and watched the news go over my shoes
with forty-four more days of spring.

                    Kent State
                    America
                    May 7, 1970

GROUP PORTRAIT WITHOUT THE LIONS
available light

MAXINE

Part 1

No party is
complete
without you.

Everybody
knows that.

The party
starts when
you arrive.

ROBOT

Part 2

Robot likes to sleep
through long lazy summer afternoons.
So do his friends
with the sun reflecting
off them like tin cans.

FRED BOUGHT A PAIR OF ICE SKATES

Part 3

Fred bought a pair of ice skates.
That was twenty years ago.
He still has them but he doesn't
    skate any more.

CALVIN LISTENS TO STARFISH

Part 4

Calvin listens to starfish.
He listens to them very carefully,
lying in the tide pools,
     soaking wet
     with his clothes on,
but is he really listening to them?

LIZ LOOKS AT HERSELF IN THE MIRROR

Part 5

She's very depressed.
Nothing went right today,
so she doesn't believe that
     she's there.

DORIS

Part 6

This morning there
was a knock at the
door. You answered it.
The mailman was standing
there. He slapped your
     face.

GINGER

Part 7

She's glad
that Bill
likes her.

VICKY SLEEPS WITH DEAD PEOPLE

Part 8

Vicky sleeps out in the woods
with dead people but she always
combs her hair in the morning.
Her parents don't understand her.
And she doesn't understand them.
They try. She tries. The dead
people try. They will all work
        it out someday.

BETTY MAKES WONDERFUL WAFFLES

Part 9

Everybody agrees to
    that.

CLAUDIA / 1923–1970

Part 10

Her mother still living
      is 65.

Her grandmother still living
      is 86.

"People in my family
live for a long time!"
         —Claudia always used to say,
         laughing.

What a surprise
she had.

WALTER

Part 11

Every night: just before he falls asleep
Walter coughs. Having never slept
in a room with another person, he thinks
that everybody coughs just before they fall
        asleep. That's his world.

MORGAN

Part 12

Morgan finished second in his high school
presidential election in 1931.
He never recovered from it.
After that he wasn't interested in people
any more. They couldn't be counted on.
He has been working as a night watchman
at the same factory for over thirty years now.
At midnight he walks among the silent equipment.
He pretends they are his friends and they like
him very much. They would have voted
        for him.

MOLLY

Part 13

Molly is afraid to go into the attic.
She's afraid if she went up there
and saw the box of clothes that she
used to wear twenty years ago,
          she would start crying.

"AH, GREAT EXPECTATIONS!"

Part 14

Sam likes to say, "Ah, great expectations!"
at least three or four times in every
conversation. He is twelve years old.
Nobody knows what he is talking about when
he says it. Sometimes it makes people
      feel uncomfortable.

GOOD LUCK, CAPTAIN MARTIN

GOOD LUCK, CAPTAIN MARTIN

Part 1

We all waved as his boat
sailed away. The old people
cried. The children were
restless.

PEOPLE ARE CONSTANTLY MAKING ENTRANCES

Part 2

People are constantly making entrances
into entrances by entering themselves
through houses, bowling alleys and planetariums,
restaurants, movie theaters, offices, factories,
mountains and Laundromats, etc., entrances
into entrances, etc., accompanied by themselves.

Captain Martin watches
the waves go by.

That's his entrance
into himself.

THE BOTTLE

Part 3

A child stands motionless.
He holds a bottle in his hands.
There's a ship in the bottle.
He stares at it with eyes
that do not blink.
He wonders where a tiny ship
can sail to if it is held
prisoner in a bottle.
Fifty years from now you will
find out, Captain Martin,
for the sea (large as it is)
is only another bottle.

SMALL CRAFT WARNINGS

Part 4

Small craft warnings mean nothing to Captain Martin
    . . . nothing . . .
like somebody deliberately choosing not to look
out the window, so the window remains empty.

FAMOUS PEOPLE AND THEIR FRIENDS

Part 5

Famous people and their friends
get to go to places where you
can only imagine what they are doing.

I was at a party two nights ago*
and a famous person was there.

When he left five or six people left
        with him.

There was a great deal of excitement
at their departure as there always is.
The room was filled with the breathing
of searchlights and chocolate ice cream
cones and private jet airplanes.

Everybody wanted to go with them
to mysterious places like film studio
palaces in Atlantis and dance halls
on the dark side of undiscovered moons
where everything happens and you are
a very important part of it
and you are there.

Where is Captain Martin?

CAROL THE WAITRESS
REMEMBERS STILL

Part 6

Yes, that's the table where Captain Martin
sat. Yes, that one. By the window.
He would sit there alone for hours at
a time, staring out at the sea. He always
had one plain doughnut and a cup of coffee.
I don't know what he was looking at.

PUT THE COFFEE ON, BUBBLES, I'M COMING HOME

Part 7

**Everybody's coming home
except Captain Martin.**

FIVE POEMS

1 / THE CURVE OF FORGOTTEN THINGS

Things slowly curve out of sight
until they are gone. Afterwards
　　　only the curve
　　　remains.

2 / FRESH PAINT

Why is it when I walk past funeral parlors
they remind me of the smell of fresh paint
and I can feel the smell in my stomach?

It does not feel like food.

3 / A TELESCOPE, A PLANETARIUM, A FIRMAMENT OF CROWS

It is a very dark place
        without stars,
and even when you arrive there
        twenty minutes early,

        . . . you are late.

4 / THE SHADOW OF
SEVEN YEARS' BAD LUCK

A face concocted from leftovers of other faces
needs a mirror put together from pieces of
    broken mirrors.

5 / COMET TELEGRAM

Two words:

Camelot
gone

MONTANA / 1973

NIGHT

Night again

again night

•

   August 23

DIVE-BOMBING THE LOWER EMOTIONS

I was dive-bombing the lower
emotions on a typical yesterday
        . . . after
I had sworn never to do it again.
I guess never's too long a time to stay
        out of the cockpit
with the wind screaming down the wings
and the target almost praying itself into your
        sights.

August 30

NINE CROWS: TWO OUT OF SEQUENCE

1,2,3,4,5,7,6,8,9

September 1

SECONDS

With so short a time to live and think
about stuff, I've spent just about
the right amount of time on this
        butterfly.

20

                A warm afternoon
                Pine Creek, Montana
                September 3

SORRY ABOUT THAT

> Oh, East is East, and West is West,
>   and never the twain shall meet . . .
>
>   —*Rudyard Kipling*

waiting . . .
fresh snow in the Absarokas
(pronounced Ab-SOAR-kause)
waiting . . .
snow / beautiful / mountains
answered by warm autumn sun
down here in the valley
waiting . . .
for a rented car from Bozeman
to bring an airplane-fresh Japanese
woman to my cabin here
in Montana.

September 3

NOTHING IS BEING TAUGHT
IN THE PALACE TODAY

The desks are silent as tombstones.
The chalkboard is coated with spider webs.
The erasers are ticking like bombs.
The recess bell has turned to mud,
        etc.

I think you get the picture:
Nothing is being taught in the palace today.

September 7

BIG DIPPER

This is the biggest Big Dipper
    that I've ever seen.

        Pine Creek
        Montana Evening
        October 4

EARLY SPRING MUD PUDDLE
AT AN OFF ANGLE

That's how I
    feel.

        October 5

A PENNY SMOOTH AS A STAR

I keep forgetting the same thing:
     over and over again.
I know it's important but I keep
     on forgetting it.
I've forgotten it so many times
that it's like a coin in my mind
     that's never been minted.

     Tom's House
     Montana
     October 13

THE KITTENS OF AUGUST

The kittens of August are ¾s cats now
and all the leaves have fallen from the two trees
by the creek that were so short a time ago shade,
and now the hunters are sighting in their rifles for:
       antelope,
           deer,
              bear,
                 elk
                   and
                     moose.
I can hear them methodically banging away at
imaginary targets that will soon be made real.

                          October 14

P. S.

NOBODY KNOWS
WHAT THE EXPERIENCE IS WORTH

Nobody knows what the experience is worth
but it's better than sitting on your hands,
      I keep telling myself.